BUILDING BLOCKS OF THE HUMAN BODY

THE RESPIRATORY SYSTEM

Written by Joseph Midthun

Illustrated by Samuel Hiti

a Scott Fetzer company
Chicago

World Book, Inc.
180 North LaSalle Street
Suite 900
Chicago, Illinois 60601
USA

For information about other World Book publications, visit our website at **www.worldbook.com** or call **1-800-WORLDBK (967-5325)**.
For information about sales to schools and libraries, call 1-800-975-3250 (United States), or 1-800-837-5365 (Canada).

Library of Congress Cataloging-in-Publication Data for this volume has been applied for.

Building Blocks of the Human Body
ISBN: 978-0-7166-4571-9 (set, hc.)

The Respiratory System
ISBN: 978-0-7166-4578-8 (hc.)

Also available as:
ISBN: 978-0-7166-4586-3 (e-book)

1st printing March 2022

Acknowledgments:
Created by Samuel Hiti and Joseph Midthun
Art by Samuel Hiti
Additional art by David Shephard/ The Bright Agency
Additional spot art by Shutterstock
Text by Joseph Midthun

TABLE OF CONTENTS

There is a glossary on page 39. Terms defined in the glossary are in type **that looks like this** on their first appearance.

WHAT IS RESPIRATION?

Whether you know it or not, you are breathing right now...

To do so, you need us–

Your LUNGS!

When you breathe in, you take in oxygen from the air.

Oxygen is a gas that your body needs in order to live.

The **cells** of the body need oxygen to break down food and use energy.

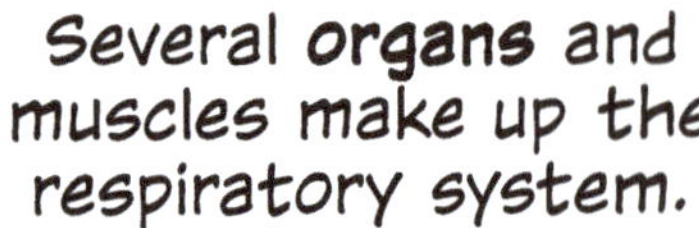

Several **organs** and muscles make up the respiratory system.

The nose and mouth connect to a large tube called the **trachea,** or windpipe.

The trachea begins at the back of the mouth, runs down the neck into the upper chest, and splits into two smaller tubes...

...called **bronchi.**

Each of these tubes leads to the lungs.

Muscles and bones also play an important role in respiration.

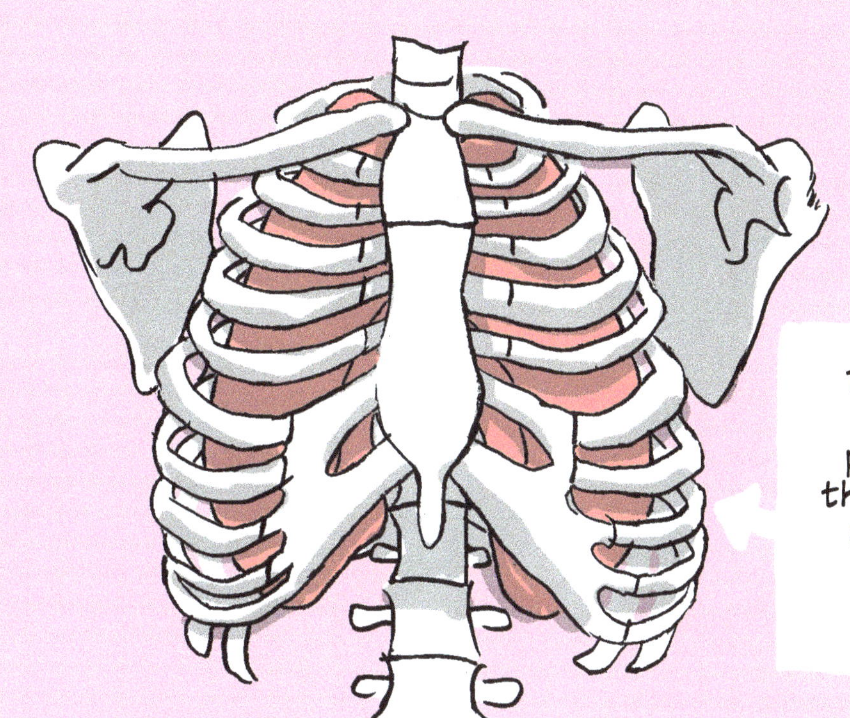

The chest wall includes bones that form a protective cage around the **chest cavity,** muscles associated with these bones, and the abdominal muscles.

The **diaphragm** is a dome-shaped sheet of muscle that separates the chest area from the abdomen.

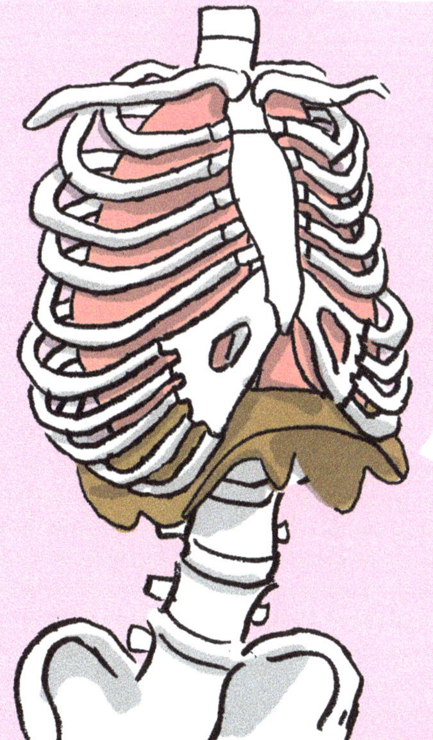

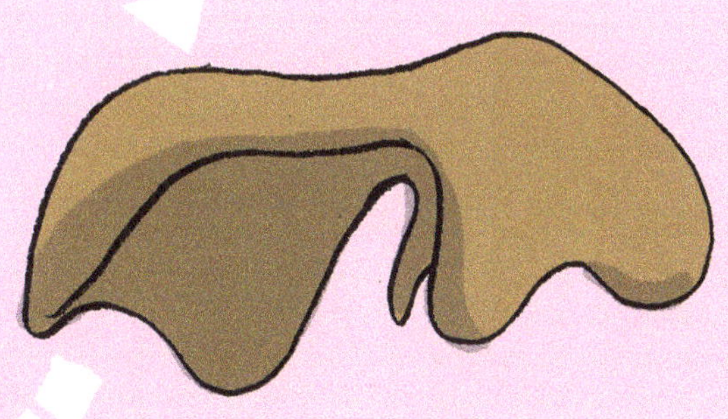

Without these bones and muscles, you would not be able to take a single breath!

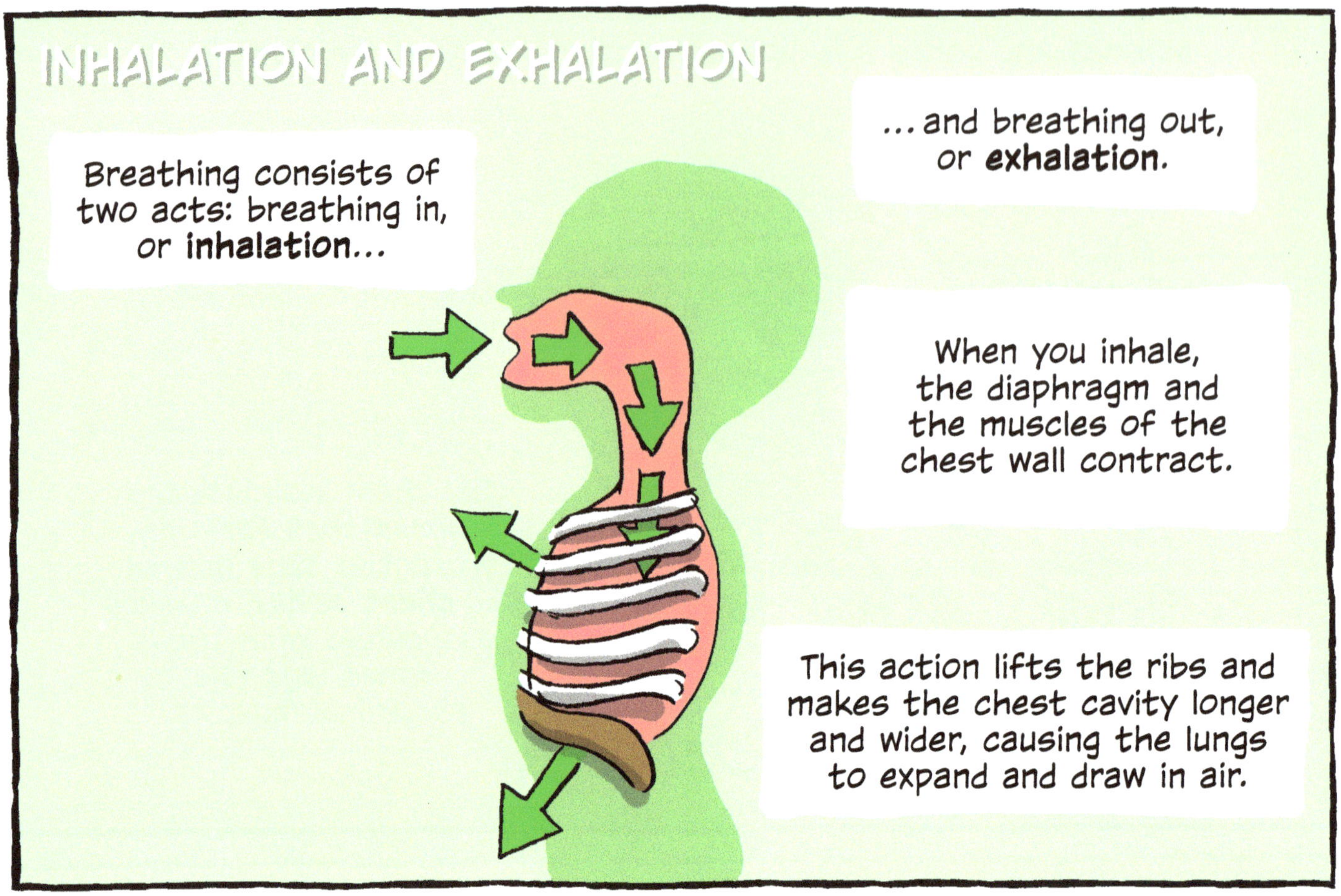

INHALATION AND EXHALATION

Breathing consists of two acts: breathing in, or **inhalation**...

...and breathing out, or **exhalation**.

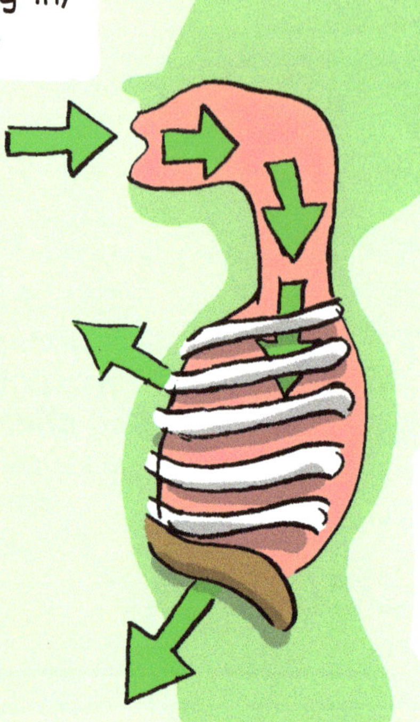

When you inhale, the diaphragm and the muscles of the chest wall contract.

This action lifts the ribs and makes the chest cavity longer and wider, causing the lungs to expand and draw in air.

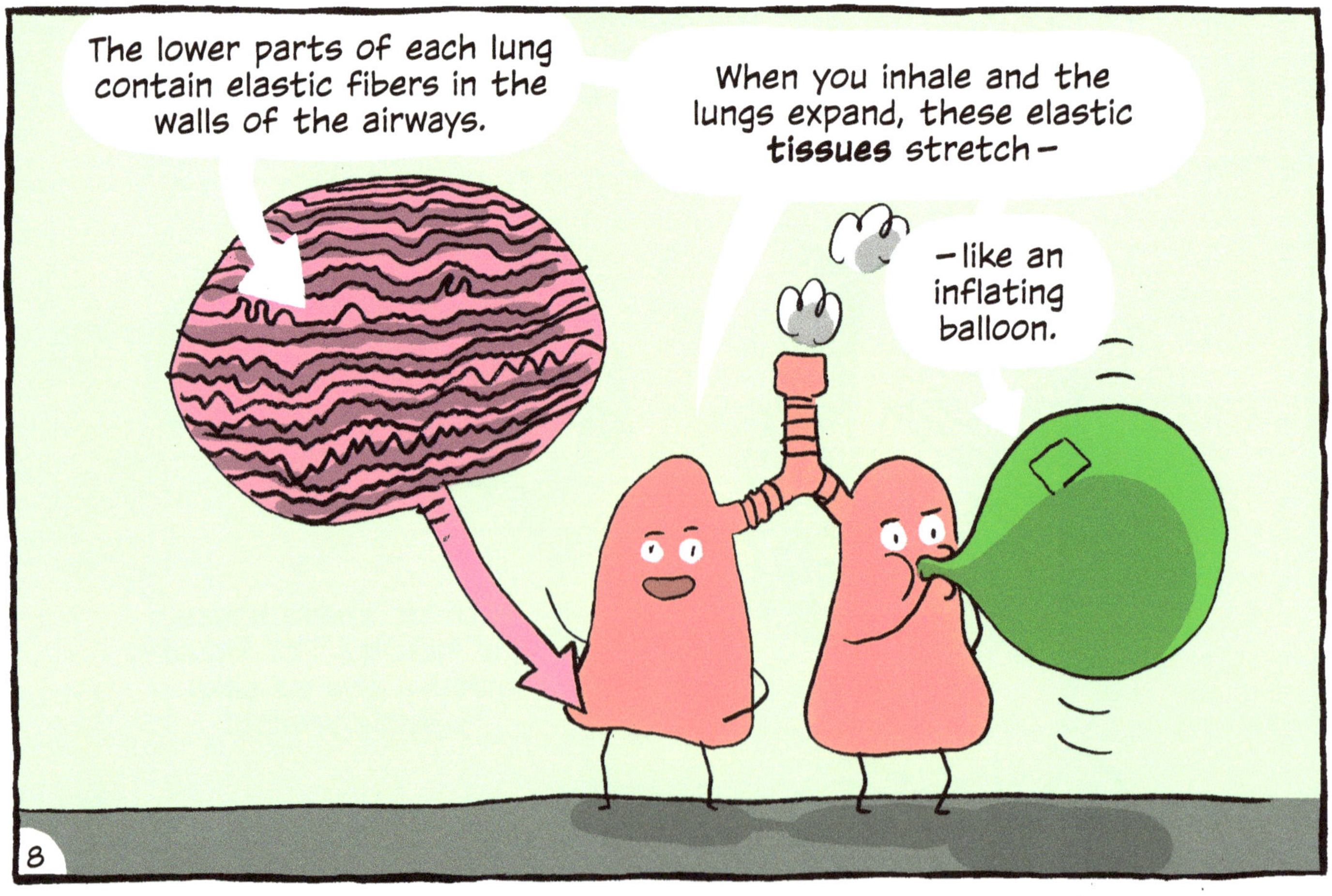

The lower parts of each lung contain elastic fibers in the walls of the airways.

When you inhale and the lungs expand, these elastic **tissues** stretch—

—like an inflating balloon.

When you exhale, the diaphragm and the rib muscles relax.

The elastic tissues of the lung shrink, pulling the walls of the rib cage with them.

This shrinking of the lungs pushes air out of the body–

–like a deflating balloon!

Sqeep

When you finish exhaling, the process starts over again!

But that's not all that happens when you breathe!

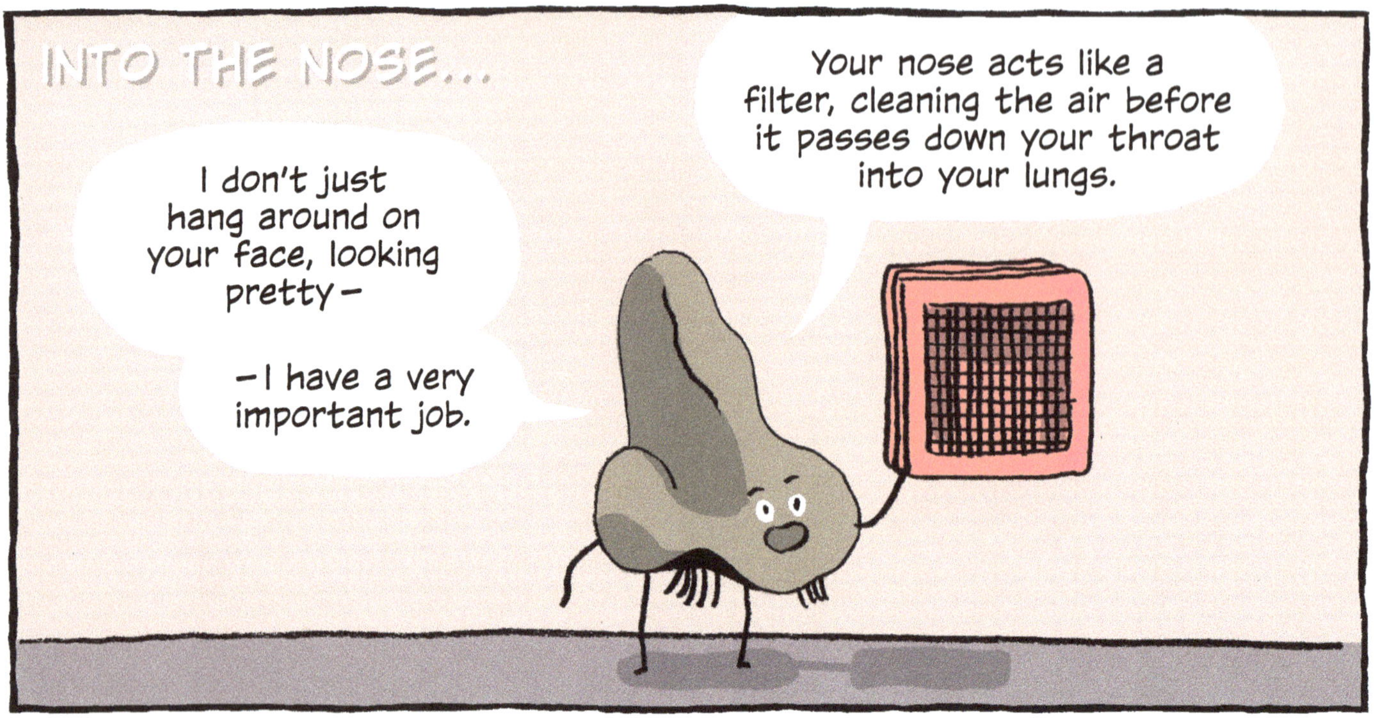

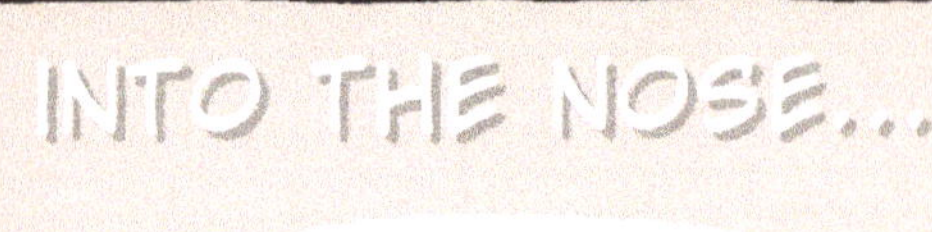

I don't just hang around on your face, looking pretty–

–I have a very important job.

Your nose acts like a filter, cleaning the air before it passes down your throat into your lungs.

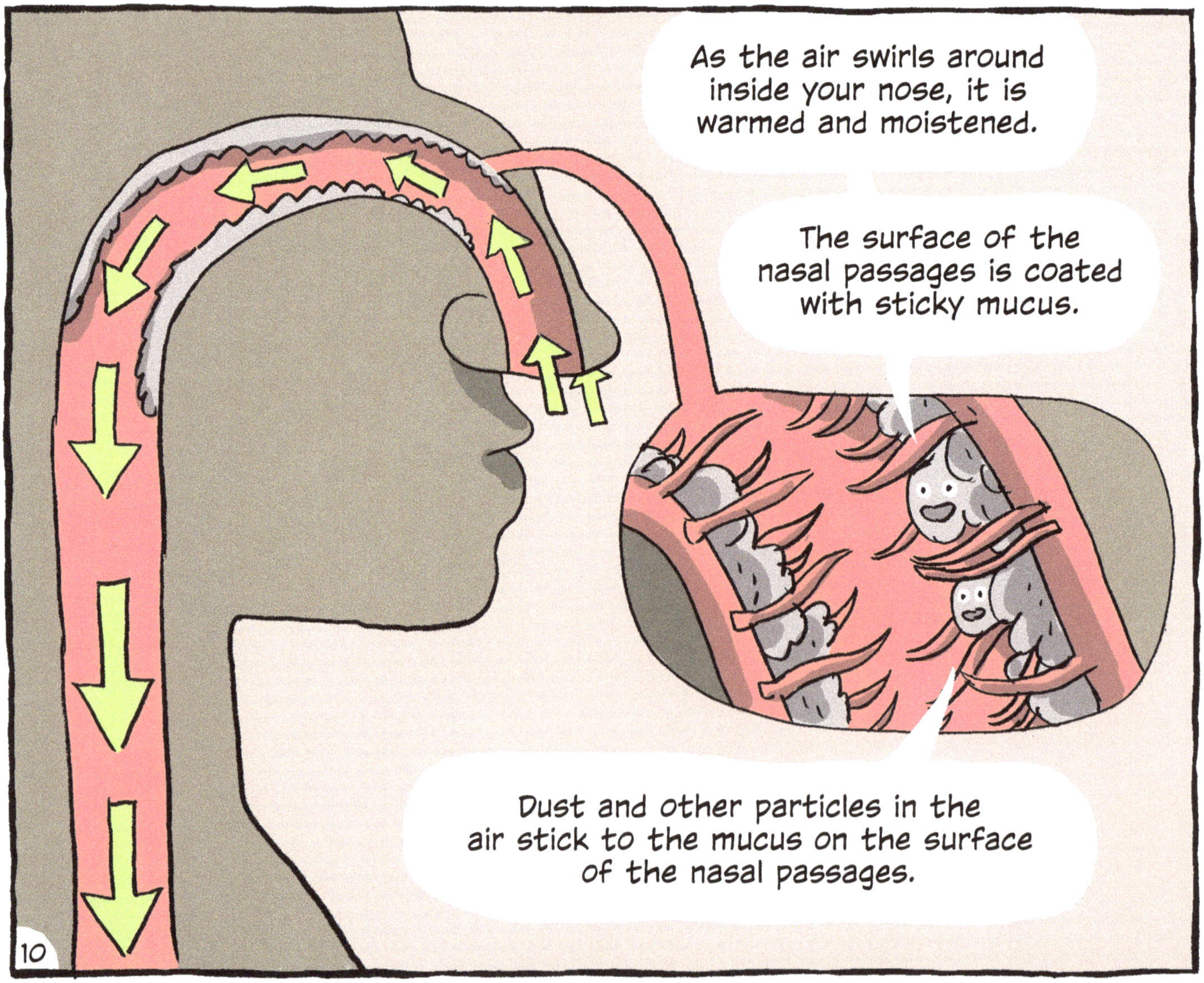

As the air swirls around inside your nose, it is warmed and moistened.

The surface of the nasal passages is coated with sticky mucus.

Dust and other particles in the air stick to the mucus on the surface of the nasal passages.

Mucus contains special cells that can destroy dangerous microbes.

CURSES!

We'll be back!

NO!

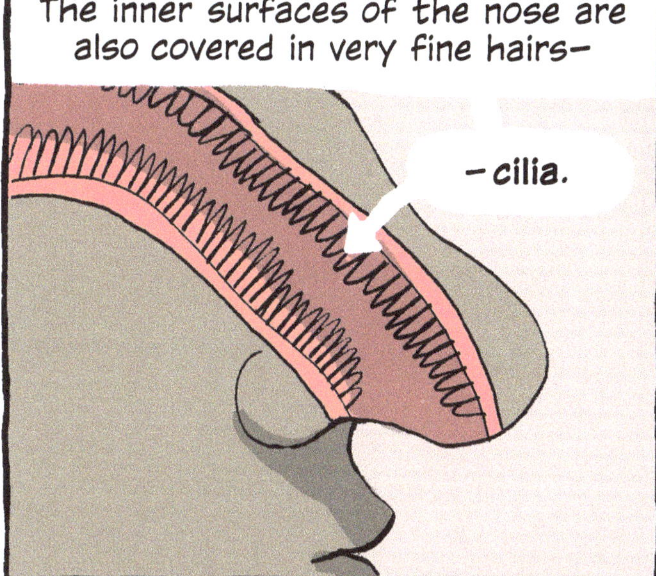

DOWN THE LUNGS...

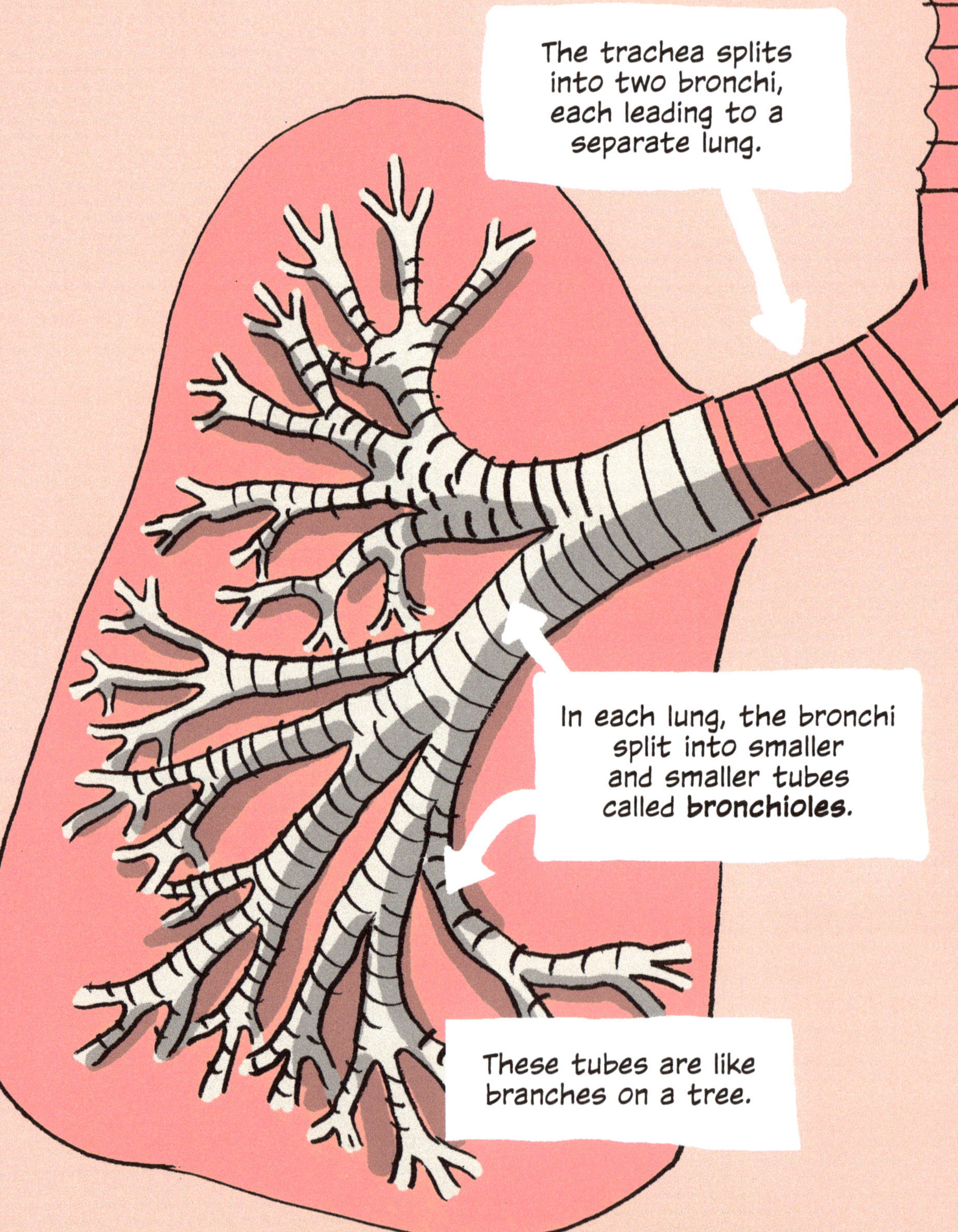

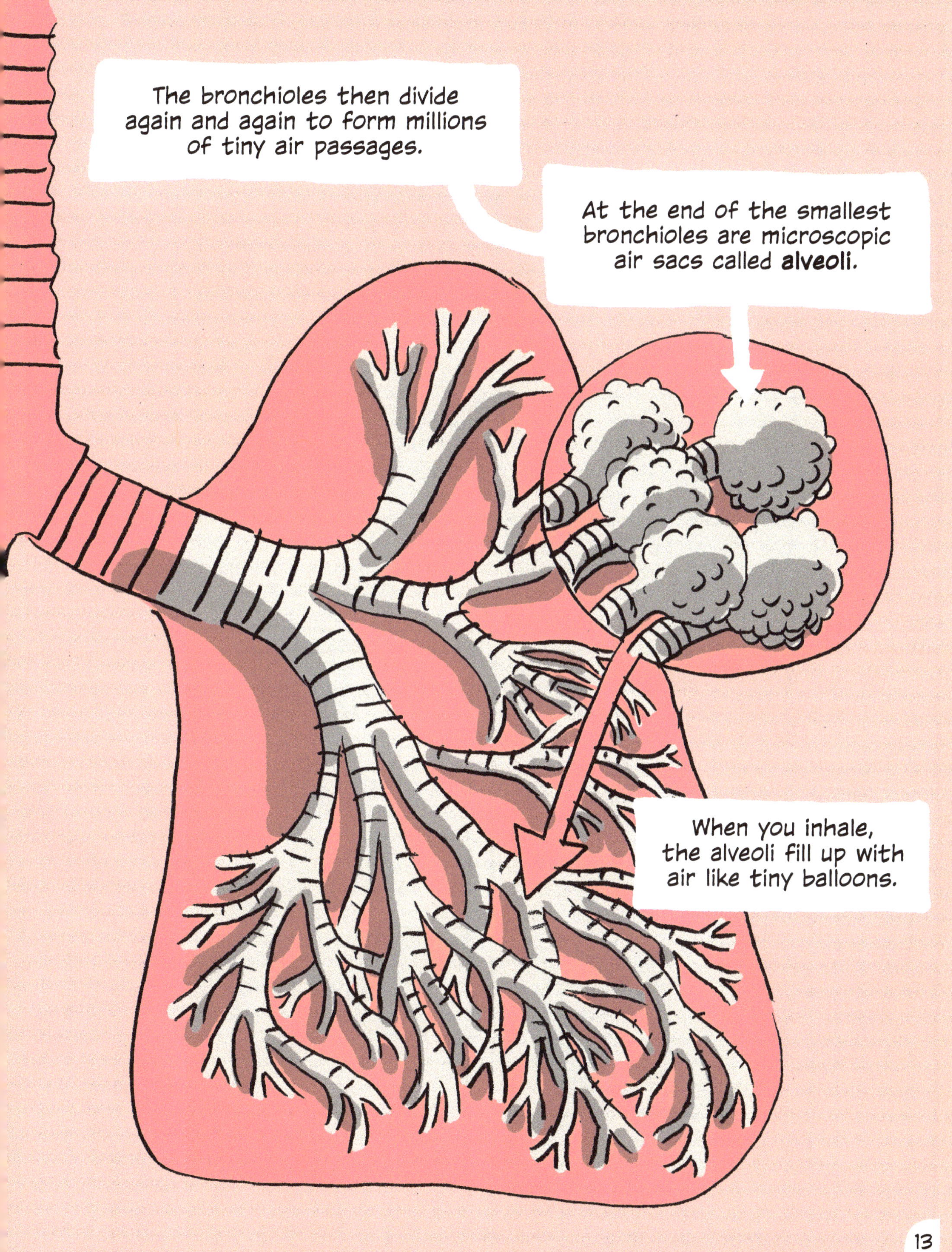
The bronchioles then divide again and again to form millions of tiny air passages.
At the end of the smallest bronchioles are microscopic air sacs called **alveoli**.
When you inhale, the alveoli fill up with air like tiny balloons.

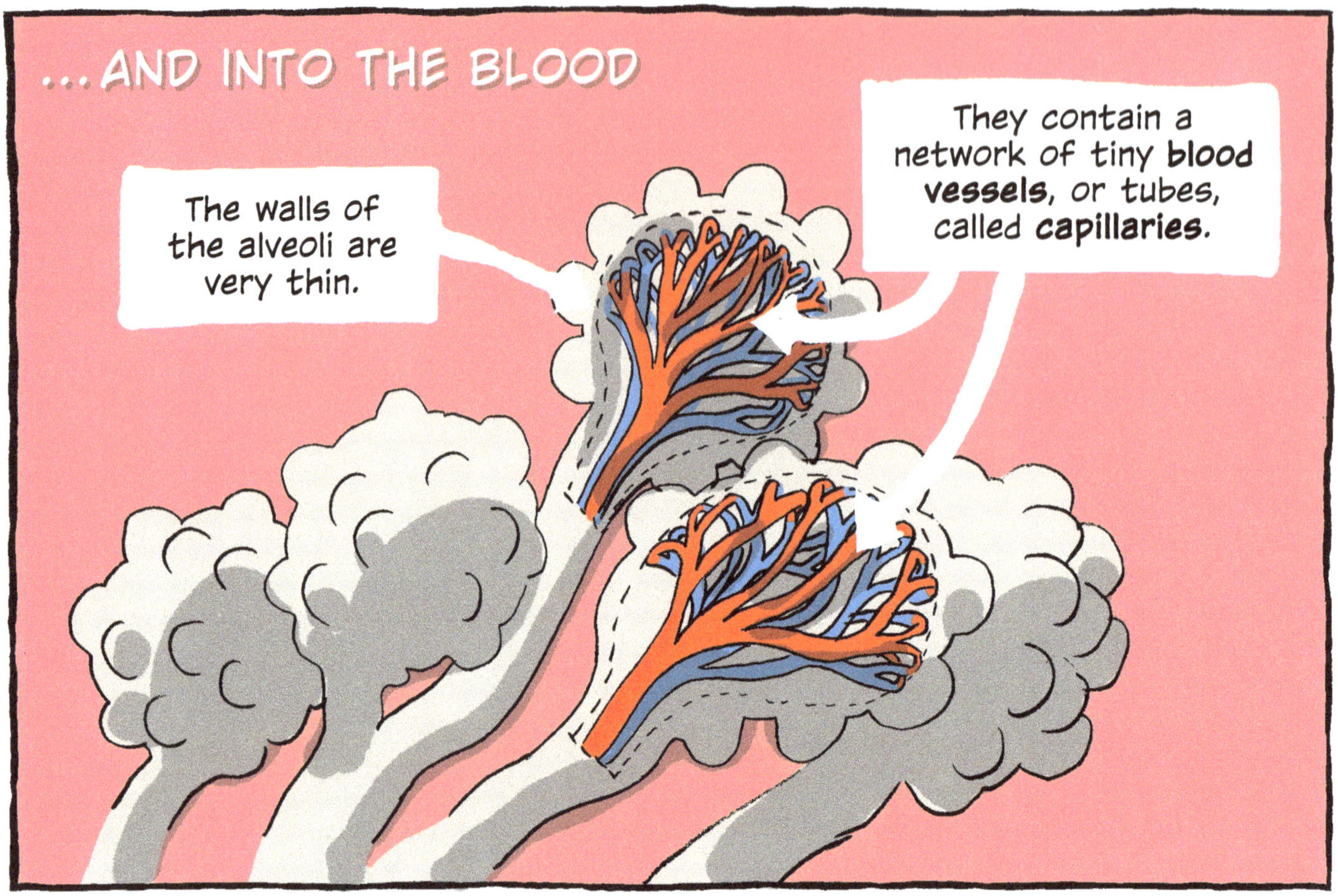

...AND INTO THE BLOOD

The walls of the alveoli are very thin.

They contain a network of tiny **blood vessels**, or tubes, called **capillaries**.

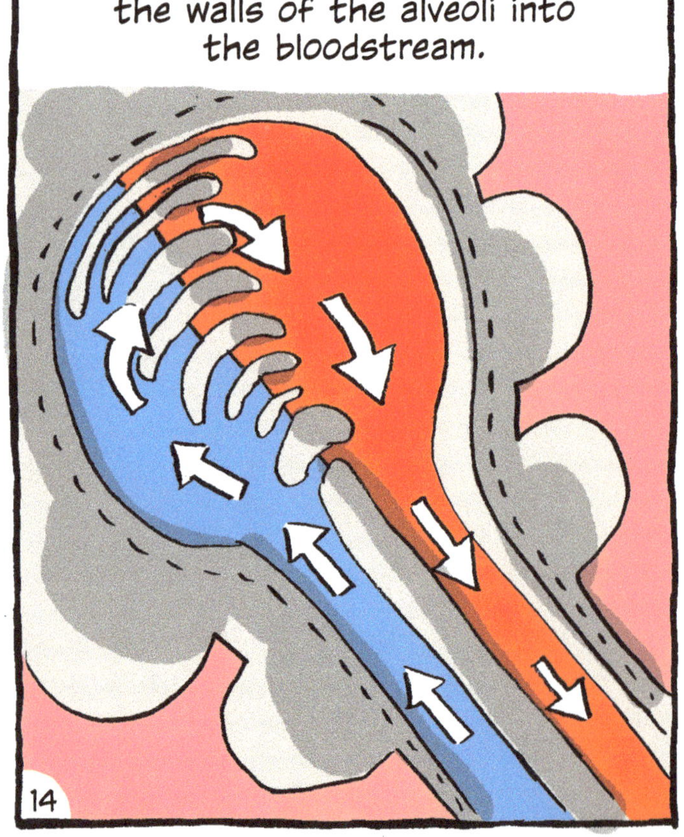

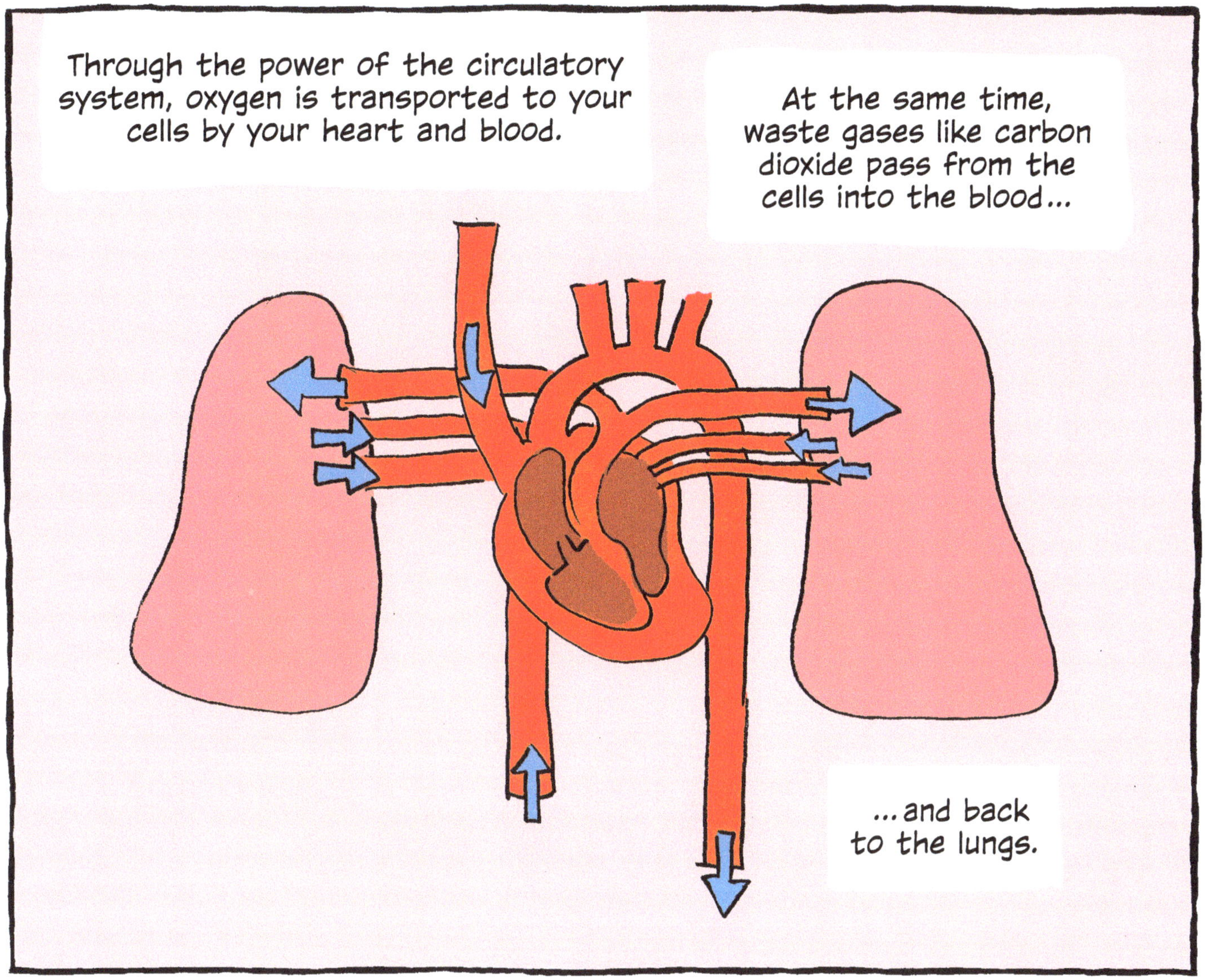

Through the power of the circulatory system, oxygen is transported to your cells by your heart and blood.

At the same time, waste gases like carbon dioxide pass from the cells into the blood...

...and back to the lungs.

The waste gases are then transferred through the capillaries into your alveoli...

...and back out of your nose or mouth.

Exhalation!

EXERCISE AND ALTITUDE
Sometimes, the body has to work harder to get enough air–
–like when you exercise!

When you are at rest, the amount of oxygen in your muscles is quite high.
I NEED TO TAKE A BREATHER!

But when you're active, your muscles use more oxygen, so you breathe faster and deeper.
PHEW!
PLOP

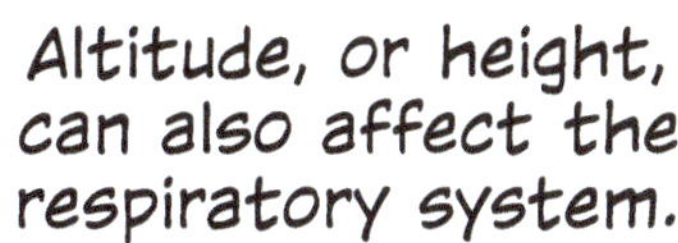

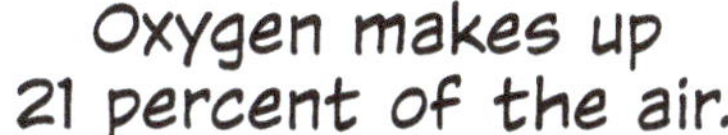

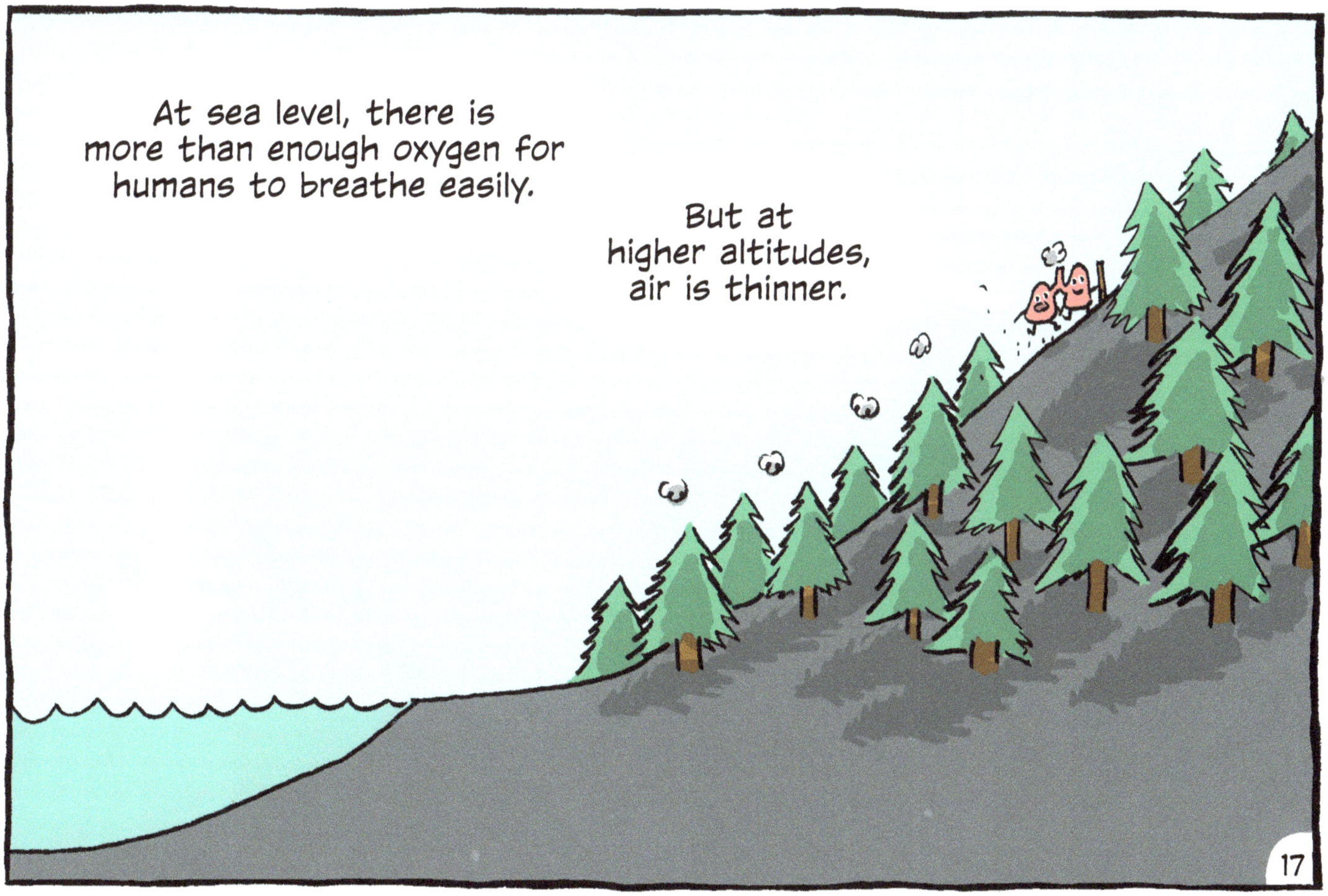

At sea level, there is more than enough oxygen for humans to breathe easily.

But at higher altitudes, air is thinner.

Mount Everest is the tallest peak above sea level on Earth...

At the top, about 9,000 meters, there is only a fourth as much oxygen as there is at sea level!

Very few people can survive the climb to the top of Everest without breathing equipment.

Yet, some people live at heights of about 3,900 meters above sea level, and most humans can get used to living at this height.

When a body first moves to a higher altitude, it adapts by taking in more air.
The lungs breathe more deeply and quickly even when at rest.
Lungs
Shunk

High above sea level, exercise tires the body out much more quickly than at sea level.
But, after a few weeks at higher altitudes, the body begins to adapt.
Lungs

The heart pumps blood into the lung capillaries more strongly...
Wap
This forces blood deeper into all parts of the lungs.
Heart
Lungs
Shump

You are surrounded by germs, and sometimes they get into your nose, mouth, and throat.

And when we get in, we'll make you sick!

Your body tries to kick out these invaders. The lining of your nose becomes inflamed and produces large amounts of mucus to flush out the germs. That's why your nose gets stuffy.

The cause of these symptoms is often a tiny **virus**—a germ even smaller than bacteria.

When something irritates your nose or throat, you cough—or sneeze.

cough
cough

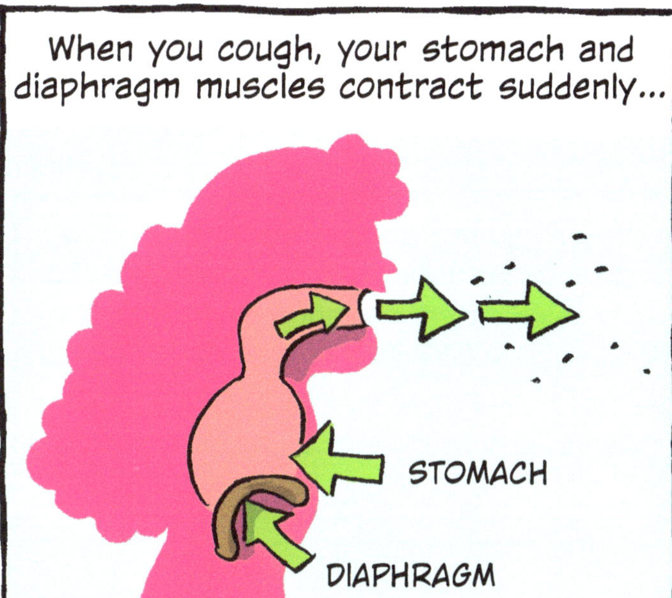

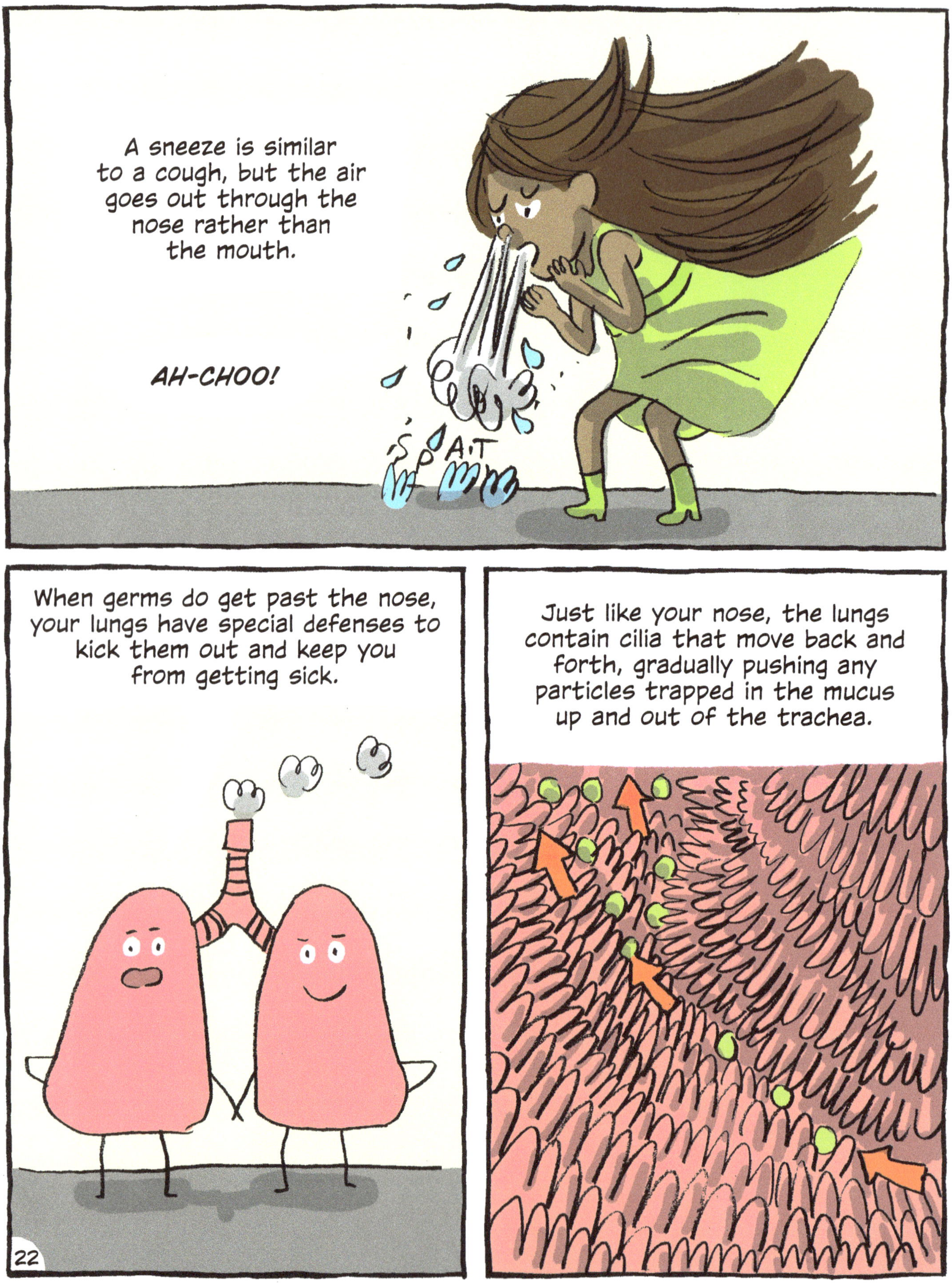

A sneeze is similar to a cough, but the air goes out through the nose rather than the mouth.

AH-CHOO!

When germs do get past the nose, your lungs have special defenses to kick them out and keep you from getting sick.

Just like your nose, the lungs contain cilia that move back and forth, gradually pushing any particles trapped in the mucus up and out of the trachea.

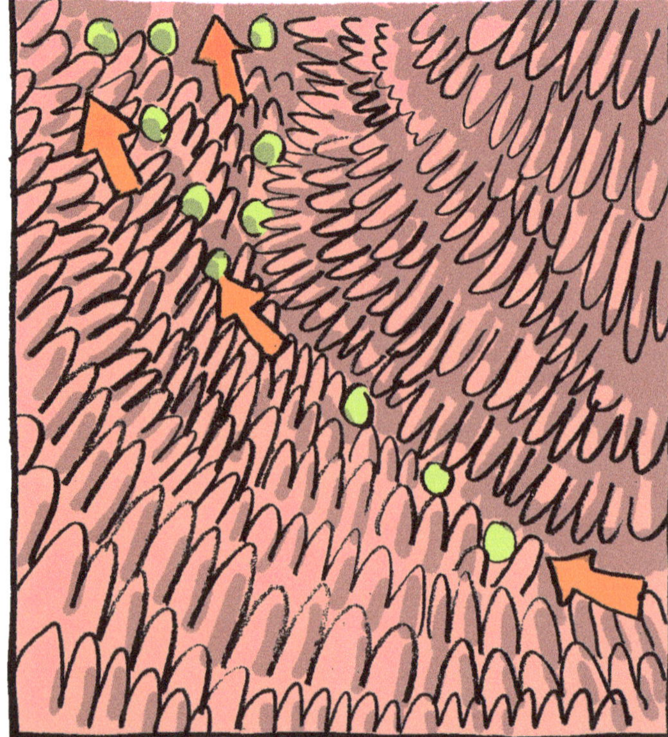

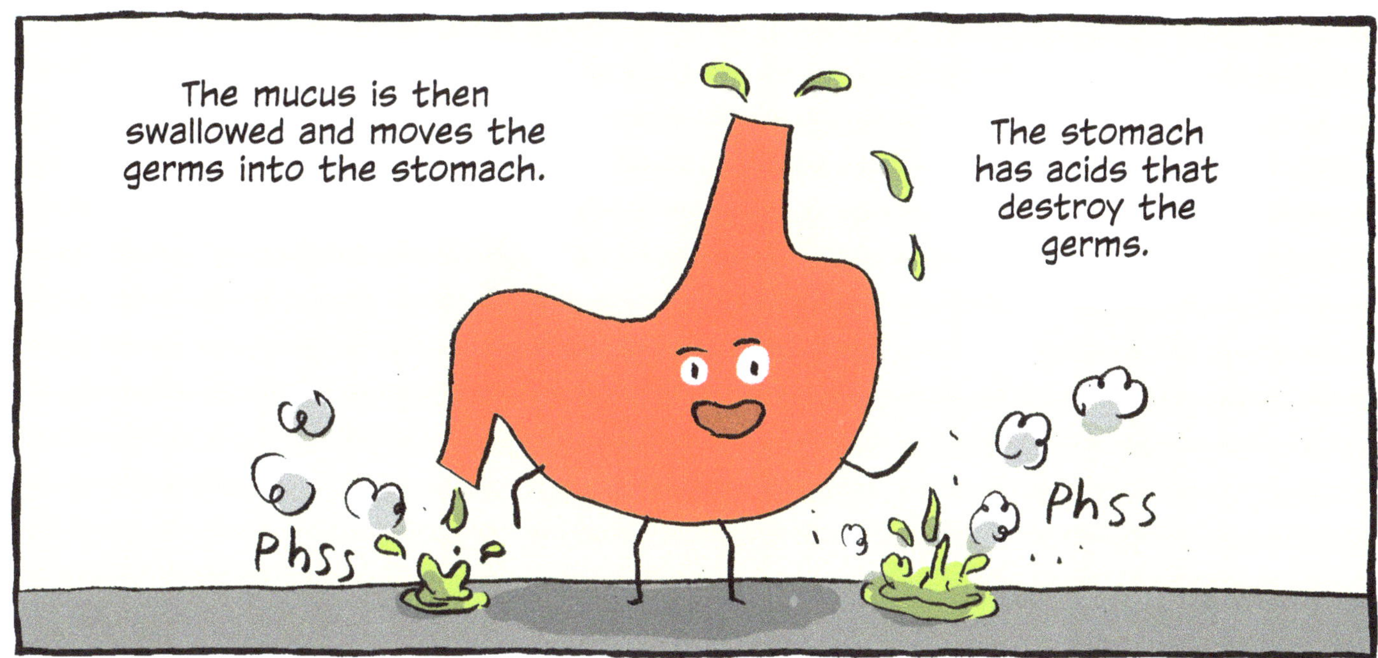
The mucus is then swallowed and moves the germs into the stomach.
The stomach has acids that destroy the germs.
Phss
Phss

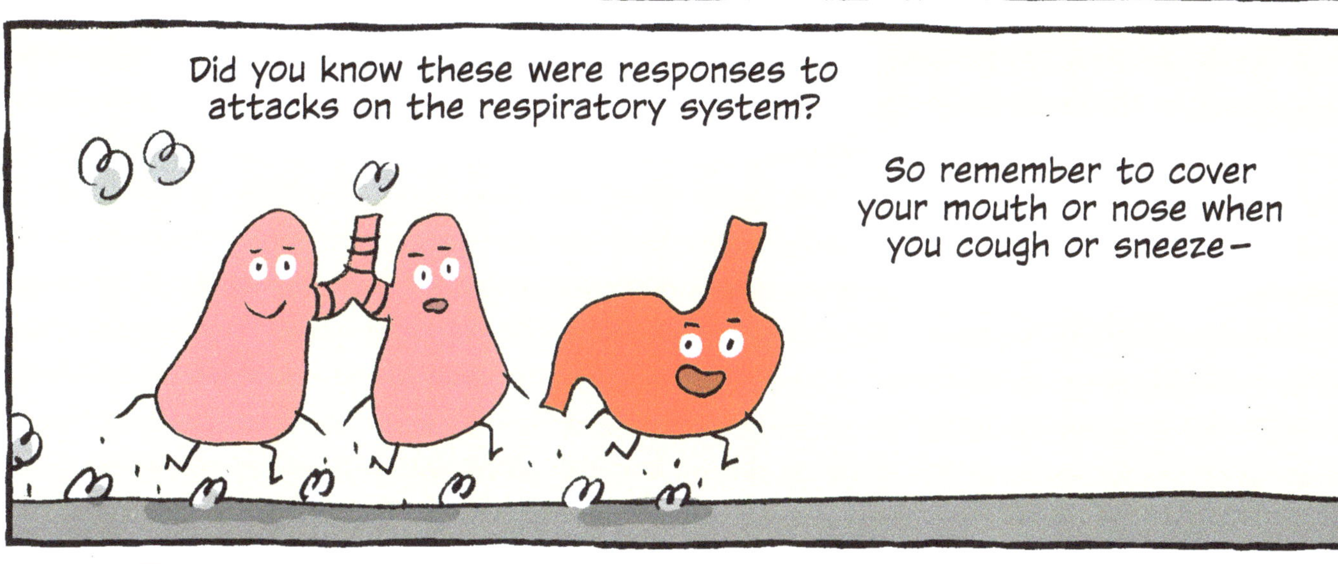
Did you know these were responses to attacks on the respiratory system?
So remember to cover your mouth or nose when you cough or sneeze–

–to prevent the spread of germs!
Sorry.

The flu virus invades the cells lining these areas and multiplies.

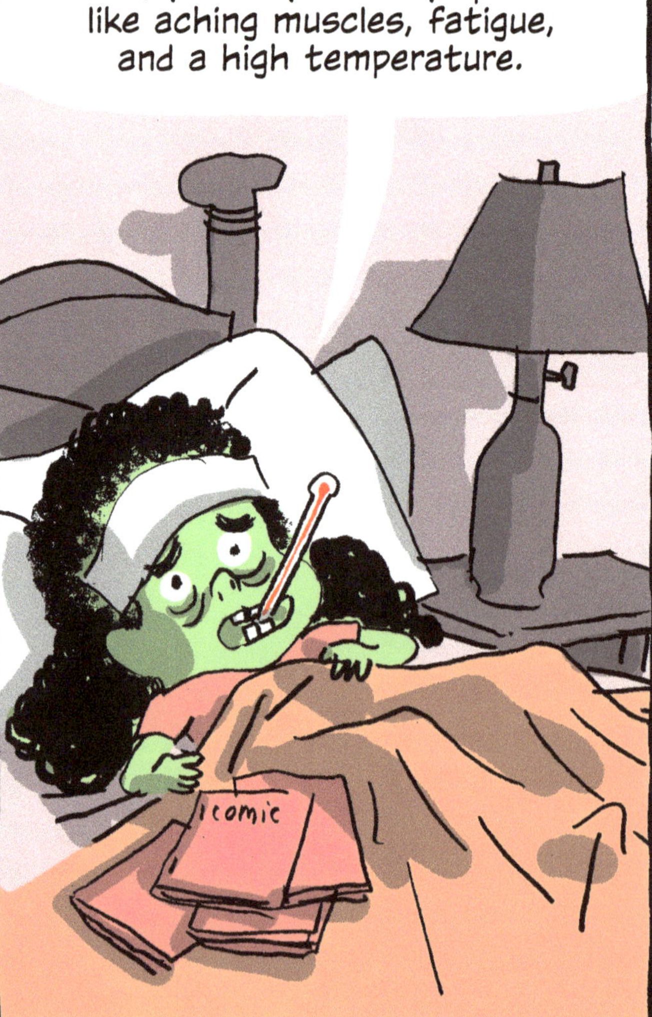

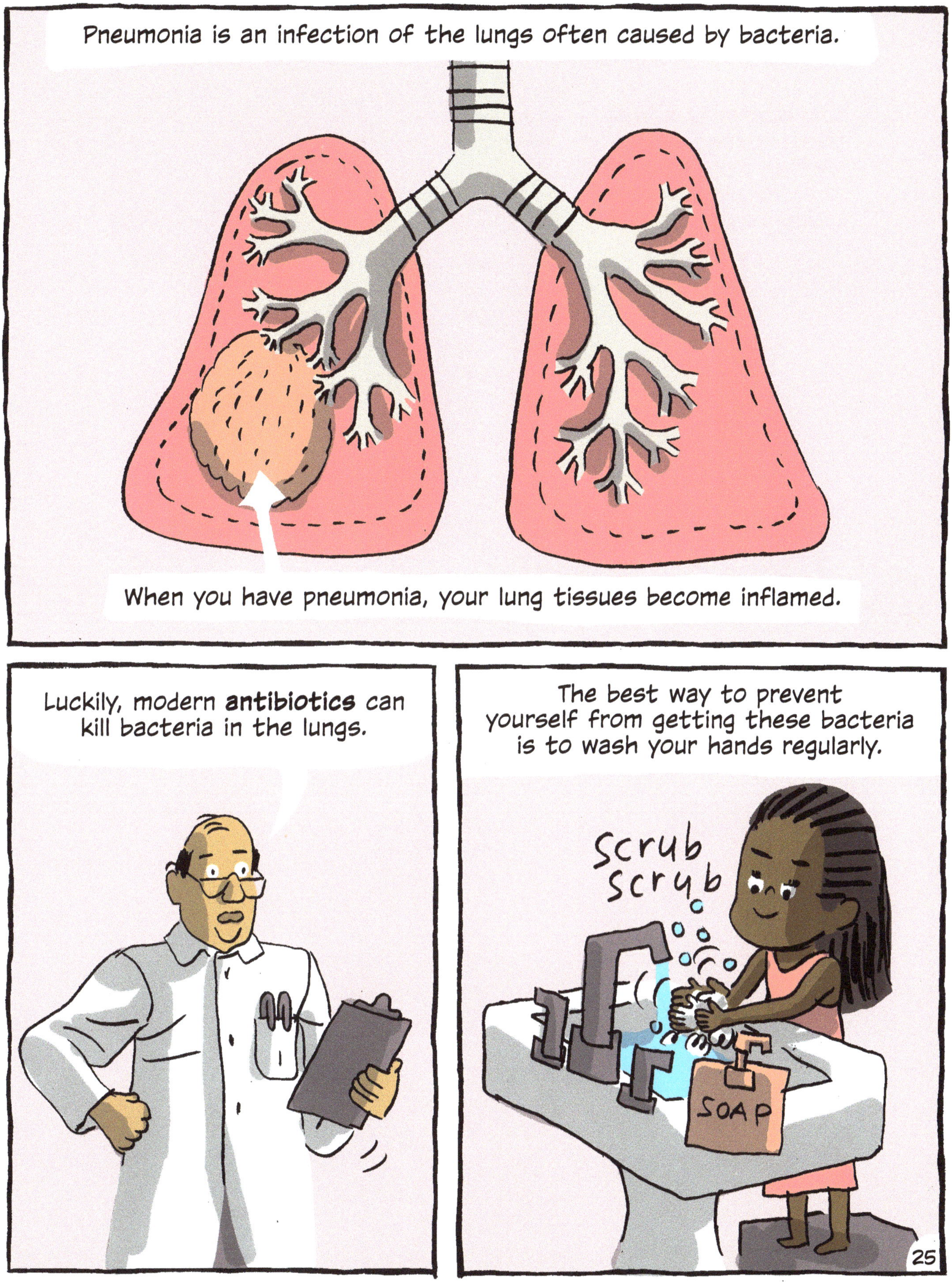

Pneumonia is an infection of the lungs often caused by bacteria.

When you have pneumonia, your lung tissues become inflamed.

An **allergy** is a body reaction that occurs in a person who is sensitive to a certain substance, such as plant pollen.

Or pet hair.

The sensitivity can cause sneezing and other symptoms.

Woof it something I woofed?

Meow don't meow.

People with **asthma** suffer from inflammation of the bronchi, which obstructs airflow.

You okay?

GASP.

When someone has an asthma attack, they can use medicines that decrease constriction in the airways.

These medicines relax small muscles in and around the lungs.

TOUGH LUNGS
WHEEE!
WOO-HOO!
It's important to keep your respiratory system healthy, so be sure to...

Exercise!
Eat well!
-AND DON'T SMOKE!

ARRRGH!
HOP

Without your respiratory system...
...your cells wouldn't be able to work to keep you alive.
AHH...
SPLASH
SPSH
A strong respiratory system will allow you to reach great heights... 
So, take a deep breath and experience life!

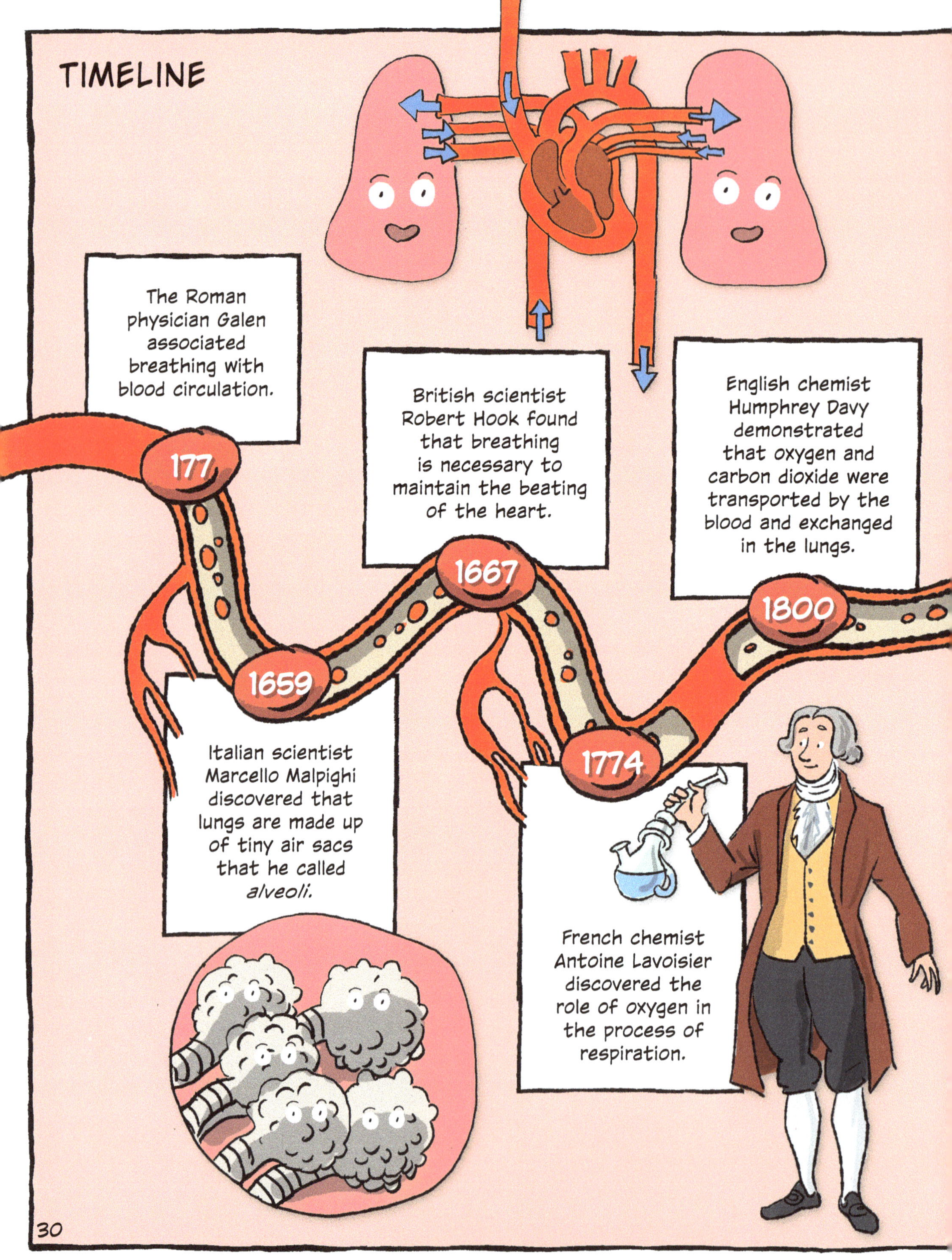

TIMELINE
177
The Roman physician Galen associated breathing with blood circulation.
1659
Italian scientist Marcello Malpighi discovered that lungs are made up of tiny air sacs that he called *alveoli*.
1667
British scientist Robert Hook found that breathing is necessary to maintain the beating of the heart.
1774
French chemist Antoine Lavoisier discovered the role of oxygen in the process of respiration.
1800
English chemist Humphrey Davy demonstrated that oxygen and carbon dioxide were transported by the blood and exchanged in the lungs.

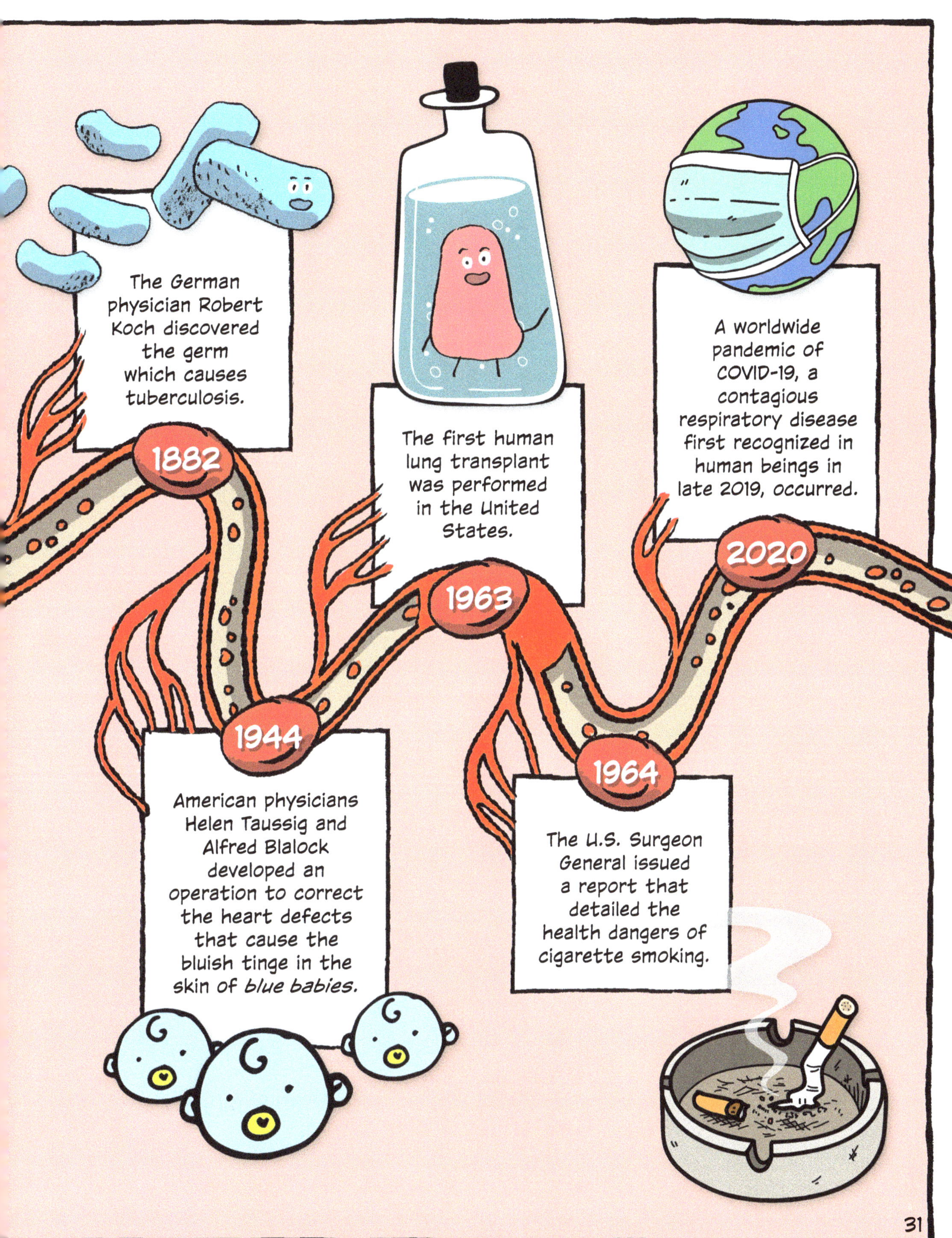
The German physician Robert Koch discovered the germ which causes tuberculosis.
1882
The first human lung transplant was performed in the United States.
1963
A worldwide pandemic of COVID-19, a contagious respiratory disease first recognized in human beings in late 2019, occurred.
2020
1944
American physicians Helen Taussig and Alfred Blalock developed an operation to correct the heart defects that cause the bluish tinge in the skin of *blue babies.*
1964
The U.S. Surgeon General issued a report that detailed the health dangers of cigarette smoking.

WHO'S WHO: LUTHER TERRY

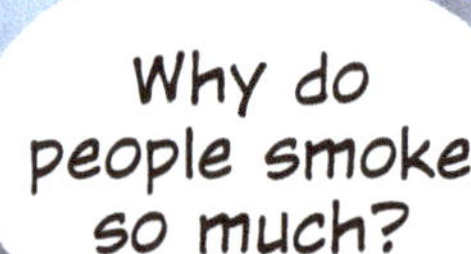

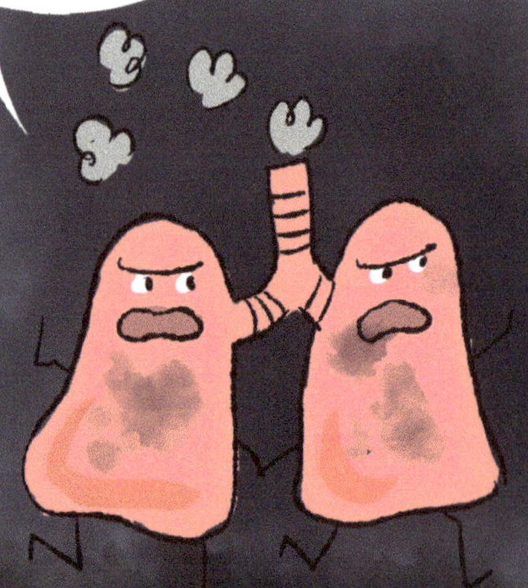

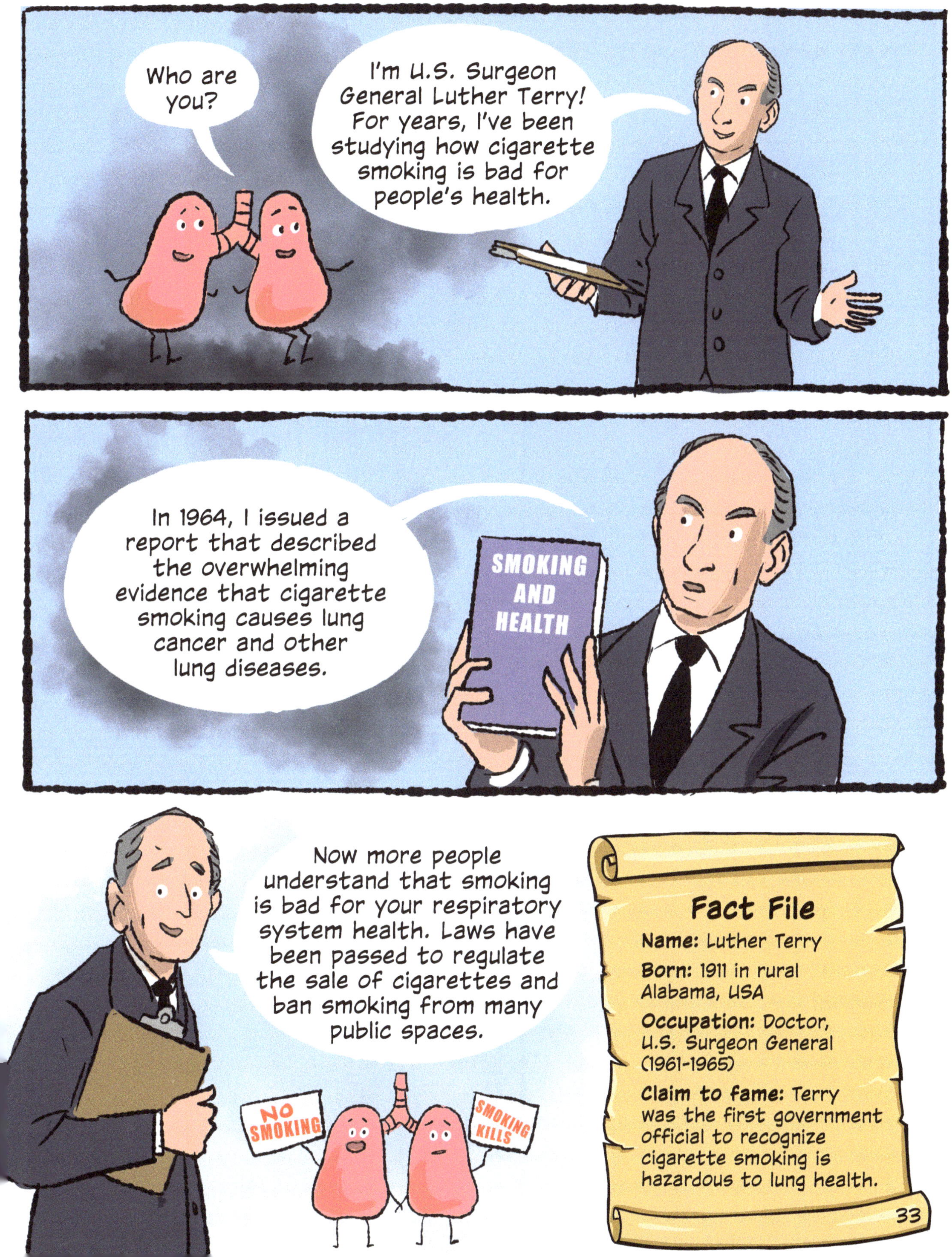

Fact File

Name: Luther Terry

Born: 1911 in rural Alabama, USA

Occupation: Doctor, U.S. Surgeon General (1961-1965)

Claim to fame: Terry was the first government official to recognize cigarette smoking is hazardous to lung health.

CAN YOU BELIEVE IT?!

You breathe out a lot of water when you exhale. When at rest, humans exhale up to 17.5 milliliters (0.59 ounce) of water in one hour.

The epiglottis covers the trachea when we swallow food. So you cannot breathe and swallow at the same time!

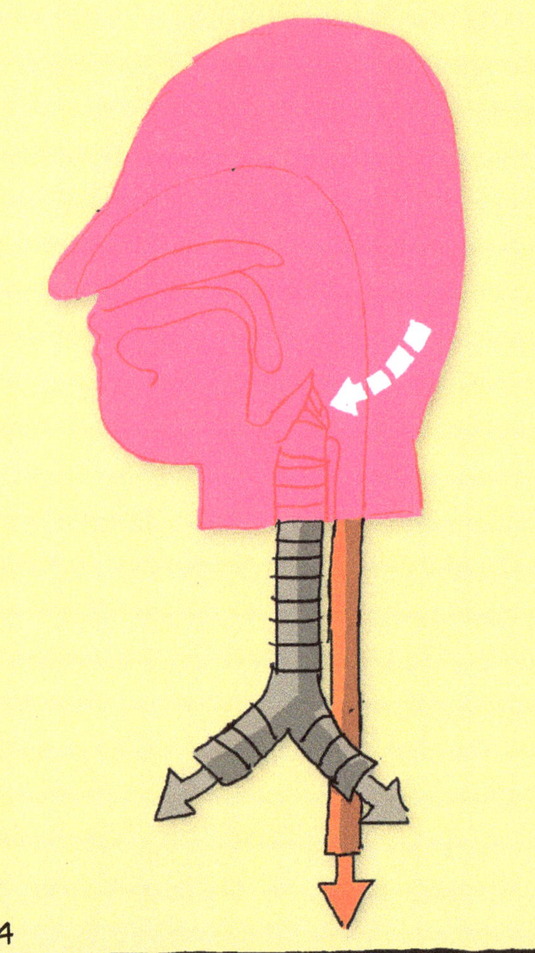

Human lungs contain almost 1,500 miles (2,400 kilometers) of airways and over 300 million alveoli.

The average adult takes over **20,000 breaths a day.**

Your brain

uses over a quarter of all the oxygen taken in by your lungs.

Your left lung

is smaller

compared to your right lung, allowing room for your heart.

The lung

on the left side of your body is divided into two lobes while the lung on your right side is divided into three.

If the lungs of an average adult person were unfolded and expanded out to their fullest size, they would have a surface area of around 70 square meters. That's enough to

cover a tennis court!

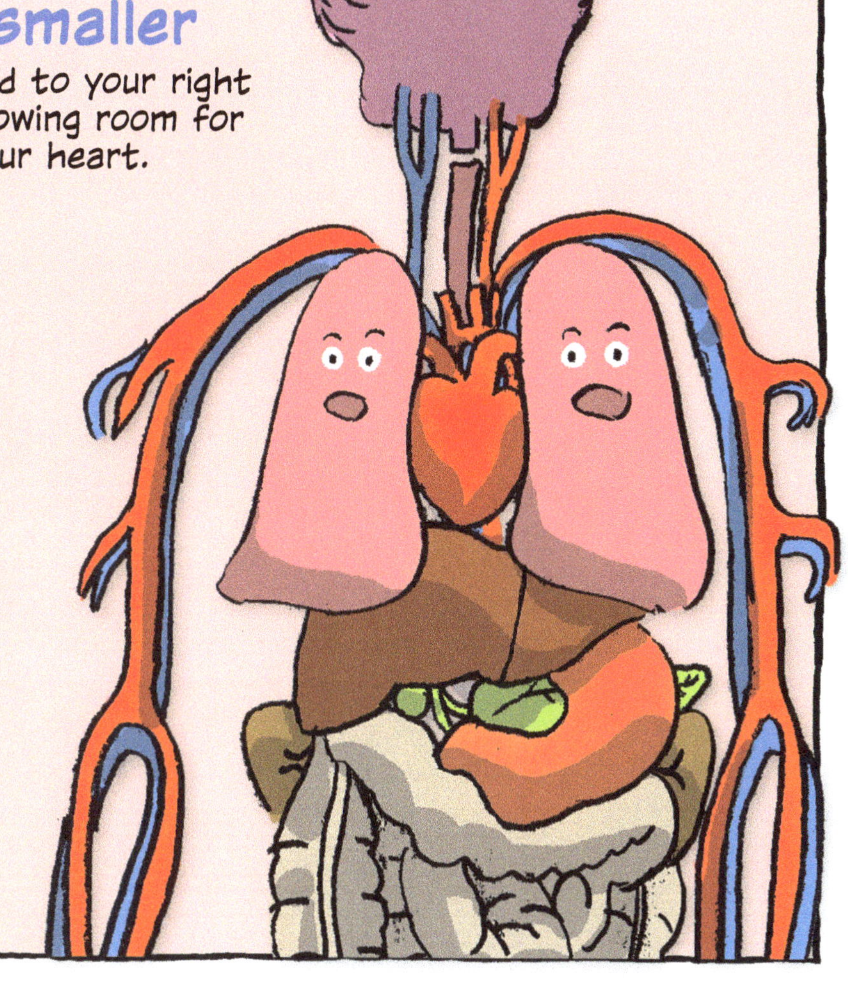

Most people only breathe through one nostril at a time. But, you may switch nostrils

several times in a day!

Your diaphragm, a flat muscle under your lungs, sometimes twitches, causing a sudden intake of air, which is interrupted by the epiglottis closing. This is called

hiccups.

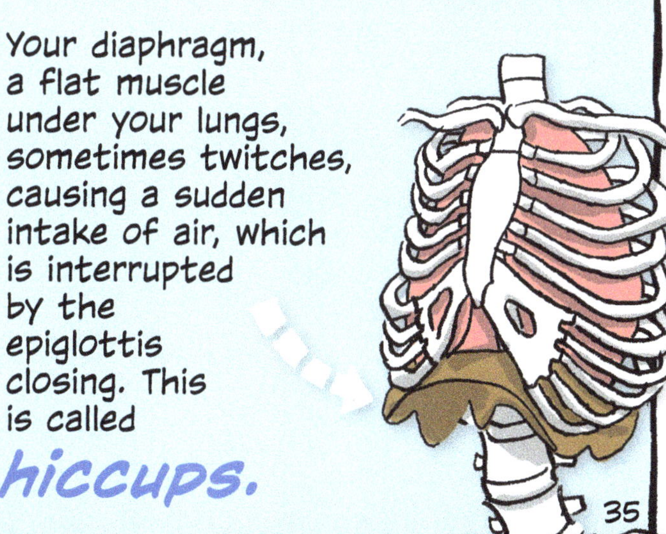

ACTIVITY:
LARGE LUNGS

You can measure how hard your lungs can blow with this easy experiment.

What You'll Need

- Balloons
- Tape measure
- Pen and paper

Give identical balloons to several of your friends. Instruct each friend to blow up a balloon as much as possible using *only one breath.*

Measure how big around everyone's balloon is with a tape measure and write down the numbers next to your friends' names.

Repeat this step two more times. Take the average of the three tests.

Sqeep

Who is able to blow the most air into their balloon? What do you think it is about the person that enables him or her to do this?

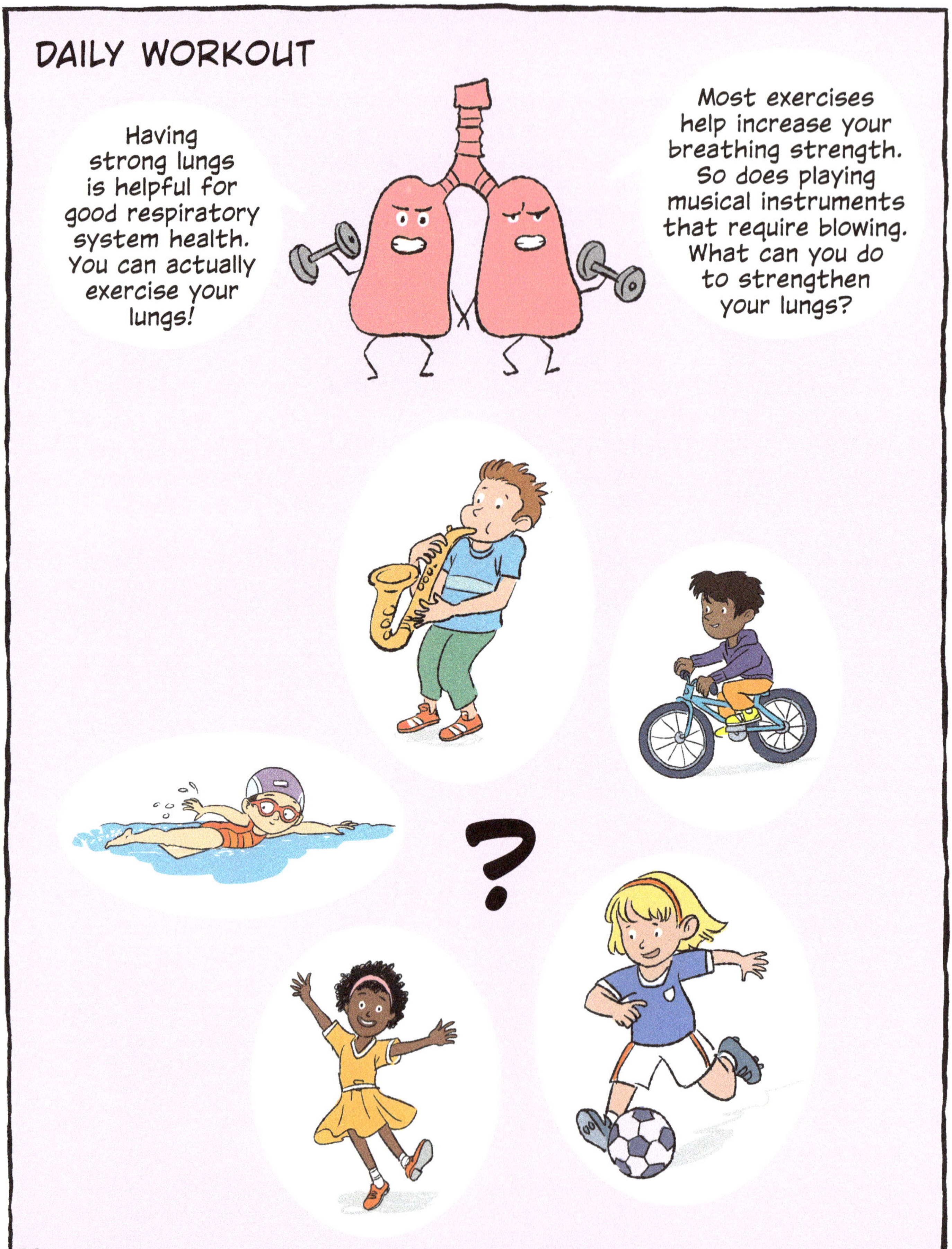

DAILY WORKOUT

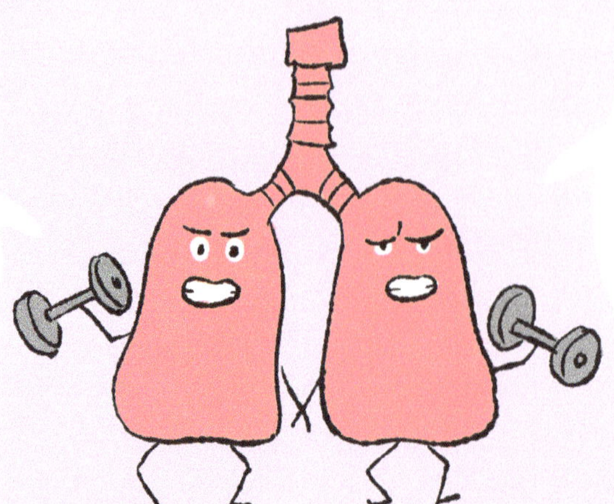

?

WORDS TO KNOW

allergy a bodily reaction to a particular substance.

alveoli tiny air sacs in the lungs.

antibiotics useful medications for treating infections caused by bacteria.

asthma a condition that makes breathing difficult and causes coughing.

bacterium; bacteria a tiny single-celled organism; more than one bacterium.

blood vessel a hollow tube that carries blood and nutrients through the body.

bronchi airways to the lungs.

bronchiole a small tube that branches off the bronchi.

capillary a blood vessel with a very narrow opening.

carbon dioxide the air that is breathed out of the lungs.

cell the basic unit of all living things.

chest cavity the hollow space between the neck and the abdomen. The chest cavity is enclosed by the ribs.

cilia tiny, hairlike structures that line the nose.

diaphragm a muscular sheet that separates the chest cavity from the abdomen.

exhalation breathing out.

inhalation breathing in.

microbe tiny organism, such as a bacterium or virus, that can cause disease.

organ two or more tissues that work together to do a certain job.

respiration the process by which organisms get and use oxygen.

respiratory system the group of organs that brings oxygen into the body and removes carbon dioxide.

tissue a group of similar cells that do a certain job.

trachea a long tube by which air is carried to and from the lungs.

virus a tiny germ that causes certain infections.

INDEX

www.ingramcontent.com/pod-product-compliance
Lightning Source LLC
LaVergne TN
LVHW060634110826
845147LV00014B/906

* 9 7 8 0 7 1 6 6 5 0 7 0 6 *